# THE
# RAPTURE
# SECRET

Blovd
Jodi
J53
Praise the Lord in every
Event + circumstance in your
life and He will inhabit your
life! Precious PROMISE —
Psalm 22:3
Roslyn Martin

# THE
# RAPTURE
# SECRET

## Why Are We Still Here?

Tate Publishing & Enterprises

Published by Tate Publishing & Enterprises, LLC
127 E. Trade Center Terrace | Mustang, Oklahoma 73064 USA
1.888.361.9473 | www.tatepublishing.com

Tate Publishing is committed to excellence in the publishing industry. The company reflects the philosophy established by the founders, based on Psalm 68:11,
*"The Lord gave the word and great was the company of those who published it."*

Book design copyright © 2009 by Tate Publishing, LLC. All rights reserved.
*Cover design by Kandi Evans*
*Interior design by Lindsay B. Behrens*

Published in the United States of America

ISBN: 978-1-60696-628-0
Religion / Biblical Studies / Exegesis & Hermeneutics
09.03.31

# Foreword

"And Jesus said, 'For judgment I am come into this world, that they which see not might see; and that they which see might be made blind'" (John 9:39, NIV). In times like these, our minds are drawn to thoughts of foreboding and "end times"! As an insurance customer service representative (CSR) and foster parent, I am bombarded daily with the worst in mankind and the world, the high price and cost of everything. It is becoming a stark reality that man is rapidly approaching a time when we cannot afford *life*!

The author has written this book for just "such a time as this." It is written for any and every individual whose heart and spirit are weighed down with a sense of urgency and apprehension; those developing an attitude of "even so, come, Lord Jesus." If you are hungering and thirsting after that righteousness necessary to survive these days, this book is for you. If your honest heart is able to say, "I am Revelation 3, lukewarm Laodicea," I stand in need of, and therefore by faith am ready to receive now gold, white raiment, and eye salve, then I say to you what my mom said to me when I questioned her request that I write the preface to this book: "Your unworthiness prepares you to respond to the unction and whisper of the Holy Spirit's call to you from the pages of this book." As you read, pray without ceasing, "I am yours, Lord. I must know the truth. Help me to believe by faith, for myself. I will, by your power and love, prepare to do and be in your will now." For you is opened the priceless Word of Prophecy and Truth necessary to "make you free" and prepare you for eternity with Christ. It doesn't matter that you, just like me, have "slumbered and slept"; we can have "oil" in our lamps sufficient to endure what lies ahead and, at the sound of the midnight cry, be prepared to go out and meet him.

To you, I say, "Read on! God grant you every miracle and blessing promised to those who love him and have no other God before him; those who long for his appearing!"

> "Herein is our love made perfect, that we may have boldness in the day of judgment: because as he is, so are we in this world"

1 John 4:17, (NIV).

Racine Martin-Hogan
Senior Customer Service Representative
Licensed Treatment-Level Foster Parent

# About the Author

The author is a born-again Christian whose life is of no consequence except to introduce those she comes into contact with to the lovely Jesus. Her only personal information worth sharing is that he is her personal Lord and Savior. It is his death, resurrection, and ascension which give her life meaning. She has become aware of, through the work of the Spirit, the miraculous promise for all mankind, "And I, if I be lifted up from the earth shall draw all men unto me" (John 3:12, KJV). Her greatest gift then is to co-labor with the Spirit in directing "whosoever" to Christ lifted up.

Who has believed our message and to whom has the arm of the LORD been revealed? He grew up before him like a tender shoot, and like a root out of dry ground. He had no beauty or majesty to attract us to him, nothing in his appearance that we should desire him. He was despised and rejected by men, a man of sorrows, and familiar with suffering. Like one from whom men hide their faces he was despised, and we esteemed him not. Surely he took up our infirmities and carried our sorrows, yet we considered him stricken by God, smitten by him, and afflicted. But he was pierced for our transgressions, he was crushed for our iniquities; the punishment that brought us peace was upon him, and by his wounds we are healed. We all, like sheep, have gone astray, each of us has turned to his own way; and the LORD has laid on him the iniquity of us all. He was oppressed and afflicted, yet he did not open his mouth; he was led like a lamb to the slaughter, and as a sheep before her shearers is silent, so he did not open his mouth. By oppression and judgment he was taken away. And who can speak of his descendants? For he was cut off from the land of the living; for the transgression of my people he was stricken. He was assigned a grave with the wicked, and with the rich in his death, though he had done no violence, nor was any deceit in his mouth. Yet it was the Lord's will to crush him and cause him to suffer, and though the Lord makes his life a guilt offering, he will see his offspring and prolong his days, and the will of the Lord will prosper in his hand. After the suffering of his soul, he will see the light of life and be satisfied; by his knowledge my righteous servant will justify many, and he will bear their iniquities. Therefore I will give him a portion among the great, and he will divide the spoils with the strong, because he poured out his life unto death, and was numbered with the transgressors. For he bore the sin of many, and made intercession for the transgressors.

Isaiah 53 (NIV)

# Introduction

"Now the Spirit speaketh expressly, that in the latter times some shall depart from the faith, giving heed to seducing spirits, and doctrines of devils."

1 Timothy 4:1, (KJV)

I was always one to prefer the truth. I loved statements like "the Truth shall set you free." Now I'm not saying that I was always truthful. I could spin out a "tall tale" with the best of them for any and all occasions. Nonetheless, I was still mindful of and often marveled with the Truth, intrigued and moved by those bold enough to declare it "no matter what." As humanity and, too frequently, in every aspect of our lives, we say we want the truth, yet by our actions and reluctance it is evident we prefer lies and falsehood. Somehow, we seem to relish the idea that telling and or catching one in a lie makes life more bearable, to be honest, more exciting! As is the case with most of us, we cling to lies, deceit, and deception as though, ironically, living the lie gives us real freedom, freedom from accountability. However, this acceptance of deceit and falsehood serves to bind us. We move in a spirit of fear and doubt. We lock ourselves away from everyone and everything. We have bars and locks for windows and doors. We have security systems, codes, and keys for everything we own. We trust no one, especially ourselves. This is not life. This is not living.

*What is wrong?* we question. *Why is it so very difficult to shake off the gloom, despair, fear, burden, uncertainty?* In times like these, with questions such as these, our minds can't help but be drawn to what we know and have been told about "end times." We are becoming acutely aware that man is rapidly approaching a time when we can no longer afford *life*!

This book is not intended for the "follower" of anyone but Christ. It was not written as a challenge to "facts in evidence," but rather an illumination of what Christ has said about the end of this age. If you worship, believe, and/or follow mother, father, sister, brother, husband, wife, child, pastor "so-and-so," evangelist so-and-so, you need not continue to read' you don't need this book. The guidance contained herein is solely for the man, woman, boy, or girl who desires only to be like Christ, to listen, receive, and follow his Word, and do the will of the Father, no matter what, freedom from everything that binds.

> "And ye shall know the truth, and the truth shall make you free."
>
> John 8:32 (KJV)

There is one great truth we, as Christians, eagerly accept and acknowledge: that we are indeed sinners saved by grace. We long for salvation that guarantees eternal life and sets us free from the burden and penalty of sin, yet we shun the very Truth that guarantees deliverance and eternal life. We long for heaven, its riches and glory, yet we shun the very Truth that guarantees riches and glory.

> And Jesus answered and said, Verily I say unto you, There is no man that hath left house, or brethren, or sisters, or father, or mother, or wife, or children, or lands, for my sake, and the gospel's, But he shall receive an hundredfold now in this time, houses, and brethren, and sisters, and mothers, and children, and lands, with persecutions; and in the world to come eternal life.
>
> Mark 10:29–30 (KJV)

Jesus here provides us with our truth, our deliverance! This is our breakthrough! Christ guarantees riches and glory now, in this lifetime, and heaven's his riches and glory in the next.

In these last days, the Word is the only guarantee of eternal life, our only guarantee that we will receive heaven's riches and glory. It is imperative that we study now more than ever before God's plan and expectation for his children. We can and must know what is going to happen to us. His Word details precisely what we should do to prepare for last events as his church. In other words, now more than ever before, we must know absolutely the manner of his coming. We must prepare, as any guest prepares for a great feast or banquet. God has never left his people in the dark as to the manner and method of his plan and will for our condition and conduct. We, as lovers, must show ourselves approved unto God. It is time we cast off the lies and deceptions that are certain, that we may avoid the tragedy described in Mark 10:29–30. We must prepare as did the five wise virgins.

> "While the bridegroom tarried, they all slumbered and slept. And at midnight there was a cry made, Behold, the bridegroom cometh; go ye out to meet him. Then all those virgin arose, and trimmed their lamps. And the foolish said unto the wise, Give us of your oil; for our lamps are gone out. But the wise answered, saying, Not so; lest there be not enough for us and you: but go ye rather to them that sell, and buy for yourselves. And

while they went to buy, the bridegroom came;
and they that were ready went in with him to
the marriage: and the door was shut.

Matthew 25:5–10 (KJV)

It is to this end that we present Christ's word as
the only Truth and evidence of the magnitude and
dangers of a great and final deception:

Babylon is fallen. Come out of her my people
that ye be not partakers of her sins. If any
man worships the beast and his image, the
same shall drink of the wine of the wrath of
God poured out without mixture into the
cup of his indignation. Here is the patience
of the Saints, here are they that keep the
commandments of God and have the faith
of Jesus Christ.

Revelation 14:8–12, (NIV)

The author's fundamental and sole premise is that
the testimony of Jesus Christ, the Word of God, is the
only standard for discerning and validating Truth. As
we ponder "what is Truth" and search his Word to

know the Truth and be set free (deliverance—break-through), we are guaranteed that by his Spirit we will be sealed to stand during that great and terrible day. We follow our Counselor's loving directive to "search the scriptures; for in them ye think ye have eternal life: and they are they which testify of me" (John 5:39, KJV, emphasis added.)

The lessons and truths contained herein are for those who by faith trust God the Father, Son, and Holy Spirit; those who rely solely on the Word for determining what is Truth. These pages were written for those who accept the Word as the final source of Truth. As we study and learn together, although we acknowledge the Word as the fundamental principle of Truth, we will be unwavering in demanding that all Truth embraced conform to the biblical standard "out of the mouth of two or three witnesses" the truth shall be established!

"But if he will not hear thee, then take with thee one or two more, that in the mouth of two or three witnesses every word may be established" (Matthew 18:16, KJV). Any Scripture we read then must be substantiated by itself and at least two other Scripture texts.

God, grant us miracles and blessings as we purpose in our hearts to know your will and plan for our lives according to all spiritual wisdom and knowledge; being ever mindful to obtain two or three witnesses to any and all matters before us, that we may remain established in truth during the troubles of these last days. "Blessed is the one who reads the words of this prophecy, and blessed are those who hear it and take to heart what is written in it, because the time is near" (Revelation 1:3, NIV).

> The coming of the lawless one will be in accordance with the work of Satan displayed in all kinds of counterfeit miracles, signs and wonders, and in every sort of evil that deceives those who are perishing. They perish because they refused to love the truth and so be saved.

> 2 Thessalonians 2:9–10 (NIV)

> For God will bring every work into judg-
> ment, including every secret thing, whether
> good or evil.

Ecclesiastes 12:14 (NIV)

Much of the world church recognizes that we have been commissioned by our Lord to "go ye into all the world and preach the gospel." However, rarely incorporated into the "gospel" is the judgment message identified by the Spirit as part of the "everlasting gospel." It is in Revelation 14 that our Lord identifies and reveals the method and proclamation of this gospel to John through prophetic vision:

> And I saw another angel flying in the midst of
> heaven having the everlasting gospel to preach
> to them that dwell upon the earth, saying
> with a loud voice, "Fear God and give glory to

him for the hour of his judgment is come and
worship him who made the heavens and the
earth, the seas and the fountains of waters."

Revelation 14:6 (NIV)

It is no small wonder that an alternate theory
proclaimed by many prevents Christ's church from
knowing and receiving the message of this Revelation
14 angel. Who wants to embrace, let alone proclaim
an everlasting gospel message of *judgment*? But what
awaits those who fail to hear, receive, and "go ye therefore" with the gospel? It follows that a great number
will be lost for failing to hear, receive, and proclaim
the everlasting gospel. The outcome awaiting those
members of the body who willingly remain in darkness was foretold through the Spirit to Zechariah.

> "In the whole land," declares the LORD,
> "two-thirds will be struck down and perish;
> yet one-third will be left in it. This third I
> will bring into the fire; I will refine them like
> silver and test them like gold. They will call
> on my name and I will answer them; I will

> say, 'They are my people,' and they will say,
> 'The LORD is our God.'"

Zechariah 13:8–9 (NIV)

Unfortunately, rather than embrace this message, there are many who will tell you that the church is gone; secretly removed (Secret Rapture) prior to or soon after the beginning of the "time of trouble". A period of judgment and terrible, frightening trouble and perplexity was shown to Zechariah and further explained by Christ in Matthew and Luke, as well as throughout the book of Revelation. Advocates of a "secret rapture" have for decades taught the church that there is no need to ponder the deep meaning and truths detailed throughout the Revelation of Christ, let alone read this last book of the Bible. Since the "secret rapture" is believed to occur prior to "time of trouble" events as described in Revelation, many Christians refuse to believe it has much value for the Christian church and, therefore, refuse to read it.

The "secret rapture" theory includes the belief that there will be a "second chance" for certain believers and nonbelievers. "Rapture theorists" state that the majority of Revelation is a biblical prophetic view of the "time of trouble" events that apply only to those unbelievers and unfortunate, hard to believe, reluctant ones (primarily the Jewish nation) unwilling to accept the "Truth" until Christ's "Church" is gone. They believe these unfortunate stubborn ones will be "Left Behind." Preponderates of the "Left Behind Secret Rapture" theory cite the following texts in support of their views:

> That is how it will be at the coming of the Son of Man. Two men will be in the field; one will be taken and the other left. Two women will be grinding with a hand mill; one will be taken and the other left. Therefore keep watch, because you do not know on what day your Lord will come. But understand this: If the owner of the house had known at what time of night the thief was coming, he would have kept watch and would not have let his house be broken into. So you also must be ready, because the Son of Man will come at an hour when you do not expect him.
>
> Matthew 24:39–44 (NIV)

Additionally, texts cited in support of the "secret rapture" theory are found in 1Corinthians: "I declare to you, brothers, that flesh and blood cannot inherit the kingdom of God, nor does the perishable inherit the imperishable. Listen, I tell you a mystery: We will not all sleep, but we will all be changed"

1 Corinthians 15:50–51, (NIV).

At this point we must pause for the sake of clarification and ask ourselves the question, do these texts meet the biblical standard of two or three witnesses establishing the Truth? Do these texts tell us that the church is removed while life on earth continues in a state of horrible affliction? What is the "mystery" described here? Is it that the church is being removed at Christ's "secret" second coming, or is it that we will not all see death? Might these texts actually be stating that the dead in Christ and those believers who are alive at his appearing will all be changed?

Unlike "secret rapture" theorists, Christ provides a clear view of final events and provides the only valid, testable explanation to these questions. He does provide for us an unmistakable description of end-time events for the world and how we will be able to know that his return is imminent. Christ never describes or advises his believers to prepare for a secret *rapture or removal* of the church. He does tell us to be ready because the secret is that no one knows the day and hour of his appearing. The facts that Christ details in Matthew 24 includes a preview of the destruction of Jerusalem, as well as events leading up to and ushering in his second coming. These facts regarding his coming, including Christ's description of end-time events, are not in dispute. It is therefore imperative that we contemplate each word spoken in Matthew 24 (see also Luke 21:5–36, second witness). We must evaluate Christ's words within context of when he spoke them and how he describes the events of his coming. Does Jesus detail a "secret rapture"? Let us apply our biblical principle to his words as we dig deeper into this question.

Tell us," they said, "when will this happen, and what will be the sign of your coming and of the end of the age?

Matthew 24:3 (NIV)

Matthew 24 can be divided into three sections. Jesus is introduced in this chapter, giving notice to those with him regarding the destruction of the temple and Jerusalem. In response to his statements, the disciples ask three questions as follows:

"When will this happen?"

"What will be the sign of your coming?"

"[What will be the sign] of the end of the age?"

In Matthew 24, Christ guides his servants through the events of the end of the age and his coming. Who better able to explain these future events? Note how Christ's explanation is directed not just in response to his disciples of 30 to 33 AD, but down through the ages he reaches out to the literate masses of the twentieth and twenty-first centuries. Praise his name, Christ does not leave us ignorant. Let us then read what he tells us in Matthew 24 (see Luke 21:5–36, second witness) carefully and prayerfully.

Jesus left the temple and was walking away when his disciples came up to him to call his attention to its buildings. "Do you see all these things?" he asked. "I tell you the truth, not one stone here will be left on another; every one will be thrown down." As Jesus was sitting on the Mount of Olives, the disciples came to him privately. "Tell us," they said, "when will this happen, and what will be the sign of your coming and of the end of the age?" Jesus answered: "Watch out that no one deceives you. For many will come in my name, claiming, 'I am the Christ,' and will deceive many. You will hear of wars and rumors of wars, but see to it that you are not alarmed. Such things must happen, but the end is still to come. Nation will rise against nation, and kingdom against kingdom. There will be famines and earthquakes in various places. All these are the beginning of birth pains. Then you will be handed over to be persecuted and put to death, and you will be hated by all nations because of me. At that time many will turn away from the faith and will betray and hate each other, and many false prophets will appear and deceive many people. Because of the increase of wickedness, the love of most will grow cold, but he who stands firm to the end will be saved. And this gospel of the kingdom will be preached in the whole world as a testimony to all nations, and then the end will come. So when you see standing in the holy place 'the abomination that causes desolation,' spoken of through the prophet Daniel—let the reader understand—then let those who are in Judea flee to the mountains. Let no one on the roof of his house go down to take anything out of the house. Let no one in the field go back to get his cloak. How dreadful it will be in those days for pregnant women and nursing mothers! Pray that your flight will not take place in winter or on the Sabbath. For then there will be great distress, unequaled from the beginning of the world until now—and never to be equaled again. If those days had not been cut short, no one would survive, but for the sake of the elect those days will be shortened. At that time if anyone says to you, 'Look, here is the Christ!' or, 'There he is!' do not believe it. For false christs and false prophets will appear and perform great signs and miracles to deceive even the elect—if that were possible. See, I have told you ahead of time. So if anyone tells you, 'There he is, out in the desert,' do not go out; or, 'Here he is, in the inner rooms,' do not believe it. For as lightning that comes from the east is visible even in the west, so will be the coming of the Son of Man. Wherever there is a carcass, there the vultures will gather. Immediately after the distress of those days 'the sun will be darkened, and the moon will not give its light; the stars will fall from the sky, and the heavenly bodies will be shaken.' At that time the sign of the Son of Man will appear in the sky, and all the nations of the earth will mourn. They will see the Son of Man coming on the clouds of the sky, with power and great glory. And he will send his angels with a loud trumpet call, and they will gather his elect from the four winds, from one end of the heavens to the other. Now learn this lesson from the fig tree: As soon as its twigs get tender and its leaves come out, you know that summer is near. Even so, when you see all these things, you know that it is near, right at the door. I tell you the truth, this generation will certainly not pass away until all these things have happened. Heaven and earth will pass away, but my words will never pass away. No one knows about that day or hour, not even the angels in heaven, nor the Son but only the Father. As it was in the days of Noah, so it will be at the coming of the Son of Man. For in the days before the flood, people were eating and drinking, marrying and giving in marriage, up to the day Noah entered the ark; and they knew nothing about what would happen until the flood came and took them all away. That is how it will be at the coming of the Son of Man. Two men will be in the field; one will be taken and the other left. Two women will be grinding with a hand mill; one will be taken and the other left. Therefore keep watch, because you do not know on what day your Lord will come. But understand this: If the owner of the house had known at what time of night the thief was coming, he would have kept watch and would not have let his house be broken into. So you also must be ready, because the Son of Man will come at an hour when you do not expect him. Who then is the faithful and wise servant, whom the master has put in charge of the servants in his household to give them their food at the proper time? It will be good for that servant whose master finds him doing so when he returns. I tell you the truth, he will put him in charge of all his possessions. But suppose that servant is wicked and says to himself, 'My master is staying away a long time,' and he then begins to beat his fellow servants and to eat and drink with drunkards. The master of that servant will come on a day when he does not expect him and at an hour he is not aware of. He will cut him to pieces and assign him a place with the hypocrites, where there will be weeping and gnashing of teeth.

Matthew 24:1–51 (NIV)

Throughout Matthew 24, we find Jesus directing his disciples to be aware of time, understand the Word, recognize events, and "go." While reading Matthew 24, we notice that Christ, in addition to describing his return without referring to a "secret rapture," does make reference to the "Sabbath" as existing during the end time of distress. "Pray that your flight will not take place in winter or on the Sabbath" (Matthew 24:20, NIV). It is clear that Christ was referring to a period after his death and resurrection, yet another general theory of the world church is that the Sabbath was done away with at the cross. We are taught that the Sabbath as a holy day of rest "from even unto even shall you celebrate your Sabbath" (Leviticus 23:32, 41,

KJV) is no longer a requirement for the church. Why then does Christ refer to the Sabbath and winter during his explanation of end times? Winter still comes and goes every year. Do you suppose the Sabbath still comes and goes every week? Doesn't Christ also say that he is Lord of the Sabbath? (Matthew 12:8, NIV)

"But if he will not hear thee, then take with thee one or two more, that in the mouth of two or three witnesses every word may be established" (Matthew 18:16, KJV). Any doctrine we espouse then must be substantiated by itself and at least two other Scripture texts.

> This people draweth nigh unto me with their mouth, and honoureth me with their lips; but their heart is far from me. But in vain they do worship me, teaching for doctrines the commandments of men. And he called the multitude, and said unto them, Hear, and understand.
>
> Matthew 15:8–10 (KJV)

What could this mean—God's requirement to remember the Sabbath day to keep it Holy was discontinued at the Cross—is our current position regarding the Sabbath. Is this a doctrine of men or the Word of God? *Perhaps another book*!

In Matthew 24, Christ does indicate that his return is *unexpected* for the *unfaithful* servant. (Note here: it is a servant, believer, not an unbeliever, identified by Christ as unfaithful, thus unprepared.) However, he clearly states that his coming will be vivid, majestic, and for the nations to witness, directing his disciples to be faithful servants, watching and ready for his return.

> At that time the sign of the Son of Man will appear in the sky and all the nations of the earth will mourn. They will see the Son of Man coming on the clouds of the sky, with power and great glory. And he will send his angels with a loud trumpet call, and they will gather his elect from the four winds, from one end of the heavens to the other.
>
> Matthew 24:30 (NIV)

Based upon Christ's description of his return, his servants (elect) will be gathered from the four winds (the "alive and remain" group) and from one end of the heavens to the other (the dead in Christ rising first) (1 Thessalonians 4:16–17 (KJV). How is it possible that they have been secretly removed from the earth, already with the Lord in heaven, and also be among the elect of the nations received at his coming as described in Matthew 24? Christ clearly states that the faithful and unfaithful, believers and nonbelievers, Jew and gentile, will be here, on earth, either alive or dead, at his second coming; and it does not appear at this point that his arrival will be hidden (secret) from anyone. Christ states that his living servants will be fulfilling his directives as they anticipate his return. His disciples are fully informed, faithfully working, and aware of the promise and manner of his return until his return. Why would Christ's details regarding this event not include a description of a "snatching away of the church" prior to the trouble he foretells? Is the secret rapture a doctrine of men or the commandment of God?

> This people draweth nigh unto me with their
> mouth, and honoureth me with their lips;

but their heart is far from me. But in vain
they do worship me, teaching for doctrines
the commandments of men. And he called
the multitude, and said unto them, Hear, and
understand:

Matthew 15:8–10 (KJV)

Christ does inform us regarding a secret associ-
ated with his coming. This event is of an unknown
(secret) date and time of fulfillment. Nevertheless, for
the faithful servant (Jew and Gentile), it is the one
event worth working and waiting for. By the way, do
you suppose those categorized as "all the nations of
the earth" represent professed Christians who refuse
to believe the "Truth," as well as unbelievers? It is certain the "nations" (plural) identified here come from
more than just the Jewish nation (singular).

It would also seem that those who have fallen
asleep in Christ are still in their graves as opposed to
"present with the Lord" (2 Corinthians 5:8, KJV) in
heaven, as is suggested by another religious teaching.
If the dead in Christ are with him in heaven, who are
the angels coming to get with "a loud trumpet call"?

(Matthew 24:31, NIV) Who are the "dead in Christ" who rise first, and why are they in their graves rather than in heaven present with the Lord watching over us? Why aren't they with Christ when he comes to get us and sends his angels with a loud trumpet to gather his elect? Why was Lazarus still in the grave four days after his death, when Jesus called for him to "come out"? (John 11:43, NIV) Who were the holy ones that came forth from their graves at the time of his death? The Scripture refers to them as holy (righteous). Why weren't they present with the Lord rather than in their graves? Once Christ was absent from the body, was he present with the Lord, or did he remain in the grave until the resurrection? When Jesus had cried out again in a loud voice, he gave up his spirit. At that moment the curtain of the temple was torn in two from top to bottom. The earth shook and the rocks split (Matthew 27:50–51, NIV).

> By this gospel you are saved, if you hold firmly
> to the word I preached to you. Otherwise,
> you have believed in vain. For what I received
> I passed on to you as of first importance:

that Christ died for our sins according to the Scriptures, that he was buried, that he was raised on the third day according to the Scriptures, and that he appeared to Peter, and then to the Twelve. After that, he appeared to more than five hundred of the brothers at the same time, most of whom are still living, though some have fallen asleep. Then he appeared to James, then to all the apostles, and last of all he appeared to me also, as to one abnormally born.

1 Corinthians 15:2–8 (NIV)

*Again*, what could this *mean*—we are taught that our loved ones who we believe have died in Christ are in heaven with him. Are they rather, as Christ states, sleeping in their graves until he calls them at his coming? Which is a doctrine of men and which is the Word of God?

This people draweth nigh unto me with their mouth, and honoureth me with their lips; but their heart is far from me. But in vain they do worship me, teaching for doctrines the commandments of men. And he called the multitude, and said unto them, Hear, and understand.

Matthew 15:8–10 (KJV)

We are learning how important it is to test every belief by the biblical standard, "But if he will not hear thee, then take with thee one or two more, that in the mouth of two or three witnesses every word may be established" (Matthew 18:16, KJV). *We have much to study and apply to our hearts by the power of his Spirit through faith!*

> Heaven and earth will pass away, but my words will never pass away.

> Matthew 24:35 (NIV)

For the sake of clarification, let us now study Matthew 24 (Luke 21:5–7, second witness) within context of the three questions asked to determine if there is any possibility that hidden within the context is Christ's teaching that there will be a "secret" removal of the church:

> Jesus left the temple and was walking away when his disciples came up to him to call his attention to its buildings. "Do you see all these things?" he asked. "I tell you the truth, not one stone here will be left on another; every one will be thrown down." As Jesus was sitting on the Mount of Olives, the disciples came to him privately. "Tell us," they said, "when will

this happen, and what will be the sign of your coming and of the end of the age?"

Matthew 24:1–3 (NIV)

## When Will This Happen?

Then you will be handed over to be persecuted and put to death, and you will be hated by all nations because of me. So when you see standing in the holy place "the abomination that causes desolation," spoken of through the prophet Daniel—let the reader understand—then let those who are in Judea flee to the mountains. Let no one on the roof of his house go down to take anything out of the house. Let no one in the field go back to get his cloak. How dreadful it will be in those days for pregnant women and nursing mothers! Pray that your flight will not take place in winter or on the Sabbath.

Matthew 24:9, 15–20 (NIV)<br>(See Luke 21:12–18, 20–24, 36)

## What Will Be the Sign of Your Coming?

Jesus answered: "Watch out that no one deceives you. For many will come in my name, claiming, 'I am the Christ and will deceive many. You will hear of wars and rumors of wars, but see to it that you are not alarmed. Such things must happen, but the end is still to come. Nation will rise against nation, and kingdom against kingdom. There will be famines and earthquakes in various places. All these are the beginning of birth pains.... For then there will be great distress, unequaled from the beginning of the world until now—and never to be equaled again. If those days had not been cut short, no one would survive, but for the sake of the elect those days will be shortened. At that time if anyone says to you, 'Look, here is the Christ!' or, 'There he is!' do not believe it. For false Christs and false prophets will appear and perform great signs and miracles to deceive even the elect—if that were possible. See, I have told you ahead of time. "So if anyone tells you, 'There he is, out in the desert,' do not go out; or, 'Here he is, in the inner rooms,' do not believe it. For as lightning that comes from the east is visible even in the west, so will be the coming of the Son of Man…"At that time the sign of the Son of Man will appear in the sky, and all the nations of the earth will mourn. They will see the Son of Man coming on the clouds of the sky, with power and great glory…"No one knows about that day or hour, not even the angels in heaven, nor the Son, but only the Father. As it was in the days of Noah, so it will be at the coming of the Son of Man. For in the days before the flood, people were eating and drinking, marrying and giving in marriage, up to the day Noah entered the ark; and they knew nothing about what would happen until the flood came and took them all away. That is how it will be at the coming of the Son of Man. Two men will be in the field; one will be taken and the other left. Two women will be grinding with a hand mill; one will be taken and the other left. "Therefore keep watch, because you do not know on what day your Lord will come. But understand this: If the owner of the house had known at what time of night the thief was coming, he would have kept watch and would not have let his house be broken into. So you also must be ready, because the Son of Man will come at an hour when you do not expect him.

Matthew 24:4–8, 21–27, 30, 36–44 (NIV)
(See Luke 21:29–31)

What will be the sign] of the end of the age?

At that time many will turn away from the faith and will betray and hate each other, and many false prophets will appear and deceive many people. Because of the increase of wickedness, the love of most will grow cold, but he who stands firm to the end will be saved. And this gospel of the kingdom will be preached in the whole world as a testimony to all nations, and then the end will come...Wherever there is a carcass, there the vultures will gather. "Immediately after the distress of those days, the sun will be darkened, and the moon will not give its light; the stars will fall from the sky, and the heavenly bodies will be shaken.... And he will send his angels with a loud trumpet call, and they will gather his elect from the four winds, from one end of the heavens to the other. "Now learn this lesson from the fig tree: As soon as its twigs get tender and its leaves come out, you know that summer is near. Even so, when you see all these things, you know that it is near, right at the door. I tell you the truth, this generation will certainly not pass away until all these things have happened. "Who then is the faithful and wise servant, whom the master has put in charge of the servants in his household to give them their food at the proper time? It will be good for that servant whose master finds him doing so when he returns. I tell you the truth, he will put him in charge of all his possessions. But suppose that servant is wicked and says to himself, 'My master is staying away a long time,' and he then begins to beat his fellow

servants and to eat and drink with drunkards.
The master of that servant will come on a day
when he does not expect him and at an hour
he is not aware of. He will cut him to pieces
and assign him a place with the hypocrites,
where there will be weeping and gnashing of
teeth. Heaven and earth will pass away, but
my words will never pass away."

Matthew 24:10–14, 28, 29, 31–34, 45–51;
Luke 21:33 (NIV) (See Luke 21:25–28,
29–30, 32–35)

In light of our Lord's answers to his disciples that
day, more than two thousand years ago, it is even
more important for his children at this time, in this
era, to heed his directives and study his Word, as these
words are Christ with us and they are life. "The Word
became flesh and made his dwelling among us. We
have seen his glory, the glory of the One and Only,
who came from the Father, full of grace and truth"
(John 1:14, NIV). We must commit our lives to service
and preparation as his "elect" and wise servants (See
Matthew 24).

We must realize and understand Christ's instruction to his followers that the prophecies of Daniel are open and must be studied to obtain the knowledge and understanding that he was not allowed to know. Daniel was told to seal up the prophecies regarding the end until the time of the end. It is our generation, the readers of Matthew 24, Christ challenges to understand. Recall that Daniel is told, "But thou, O Daniel, shut up the words, and seal the book, even to the time of the end: many shall run to and fro, *and knowledge shall be increased*" (Daniel 12:4, KJV, emphasis added). Thus, it is Christ himself who opens the prophecies of Daniel. It is Christ who informs us that the "unsealing" of Daniel's prophecy of last-day events occurs at the time when his followers have access to and are able to "read" Matthew 24! "So when you see standing in the holy place 'the abomination that causes desolation,' spoken of through the prophet Daniel—let the reader understand..."

As we "read" Matthew 24, we should now understand that our Lord was speaking through time directly to this generation of global print, audio, and visual media—this era when the majority of the world has access to and can "read" his words. We should recognize that decades before his words were written, Christ prophetically speaks to our generation of believers, detailing final events and instructing us where to turn in his Word for guidance and clarity. At the time he spoke these words, the world, the masses, even some of his followers present that day, were illiterate. Centuries would pass before the reformation and technology would make his words available for believers to actually "read" for themselves.

The question that remains for us—will we embrace the second part of his admonition—will we understand?

> And this gospel of the kingdom will be preached in the whole world as a testimony to all nations, and then the end will come. So when you see standing in the holy place the abomination that causes desolation, spoken of through the prophet Daniel—let the reader understand.
>
> Matthew 24:14 (NIV)

It appears the Word is stating that anyone who can read Christ's words should understand time, kingdom, and end-time prophecies of Daniel.

Studying Daniel to understand necessarily leads us to study Revelation, as both books refer to the kingdoms of the earth, the oppression of God's people and his Word, the time of trouble, the vindication of God's people and his Word, and our Lord's return. The time is now, as the whole world has access and ability to read the Word for oneself. Knowing this, we must ask for and receive the Holy Spirit's guidance and understanding! Simply put, there is now a light of love available to the entire world to illuminate our way to understand the time and the truth. We must prepare. We must be prepared.

Understanding now that Christ's words (Matthew 24) were intended for us, a world capable of preaching this gospel to the whole world and capable of reading his Word for ourselves (Matthew 24:14), aren't we the generation challenged to "understand" end time events; as well the meaning of what the world is going through now (politics, economics, war, terrorism, the challenges to "buying and selling")? Christ, as he describes his coming throughout Matthew 24, declares that his angels will be sent to gather his elect from the four winds in the presence of all the nations of the earth. He describes several signs to appear in the sky and explains that all nations of the earth mourn. It is Christ himself who states that all will see him in the clouds and tells us that he will send his angels to gather the believers. Finally, Jesus states that his return to receive his followers will be accompanied by a loud trumpet call! Matthew 24:30–31 (NIV).

*Once again, where's the secret!* The church, his followers, his elect are still here on earth awaiting his return in faithful, informed obedience. Question— was Christ, is Christ describing twenty-first-century earth?

4

And ye shall know the truth, and the truth
shall make you free.

John 8:32 (KJV)

Based upon texts cited in the preceding chapters, and
realizing that Christ directs readers to understand
time and kingdom prophecies as these events unfold,
it is imperative that we explore what the Word records
regarding a "secret" manner and nature of his coming.
Can we find any reference to substantiate that these
events should be interpreted as Christ secretly remov-
ing his "elect" away prior to the troubles identified
by Daniel and John the Revelator, as well as those
described in both Matthew 24 and Luke 21? Utilizing
Internet-based "Gospelnet.com" Bible study resources,
a "keyword" search for the word "rapture" in various
versions of the Bible resulted in the following:

**Quick Search Results**

Showing results from: | King James Version ▼ |

Keyword search results

0 Results

Sorry. No results found for "rapture" in Keyword Search.

Topical index results

0 Results

Sorry. No results found for "rapture" in Topical Index.

**Quick Search Results**

Showing results from: | New King James Version ▼ |

Keyword search results

0 Results

Sorry. No results found for "rapture" in Keyword Search.

Topical index results

0 Results

Sorry. No results found for "rapture" in Topical Index.

**Quick Search Results**

Showing results from: | New International Version ▼ |

Keyword search results

0 Results

Sorry. No results found for "rapture" in Keyword Search.

Topical index results

0 Results

Sorry. No results found for "rapture" in Topical Index.

## Quick Search Results

Showing results from: `American Standard Version ▾`

Keyword search results

0 Results

Sorry. No results found for "rapture" in Keyword Search.

Topical index results

0 Results

Sorry. No results found for "rapture" in Topical Index.

## Quick Search Results

Showing results from: `New American Standard Bible ▾`

Keyword search results

0 Results

Sorry. No results found for "rapture" in Keyword Search.

Topical index results

0 Results

Sorry. No results found for "rapture" in Topical Index.

## Quick Search Results

Showing results from: | New Living Translation ▼ |

Keyword search results

0 Results

Sorry. No results found for "rapture" in Keyword Search.

Topical index results

0 Results

Sorry. No results found for "rapture" in Topical Index.


## Quick Search Results

Showing results from: | Amplified Bible ▼ |

Keyword search results

1 Results

0 Results

Sorry. No results found for "rapture" in Topical Index.


Only one version contains a term identified as *synonymous* with "rapture." Please note, the word "rapture" neither appears in this version, nor is it contained within the actual text. Additionally, this reference states nothing regarding the secret removal of the church prior to the end time of trouble or the end-time events depicted in Daniel and Revelation.

The word "rapture" is not written anywhere in God's Word. We have also discovered that it is never used by Christ, nor does he make reference to a secret removal of the church before or at his second coming and prior to the end time of trouble.

Not finding the term "rapture" in the Bible, let us turn to standard English-language resources to determine if by definition we can trace a definitive reason to consider the meaning of "rapture" as synonymous with a secret removal of the church. Can we find support for a religious principle espousing the theory that there will be a first-stage redemptive event resulting in the body of Christ, the church being secretly removed from this earth? Can we find linguistic justification for the theory of a salvation "second chance" and second-stage redemptive event for Jewish and reluctant believers, after which, the destruction of Satan and all evil?

In the *Merriam-Webster Dictionary*, I found the following entry:

Main Entry: *rap·ture*
Pronunciation: 'rap-ch&r
Function: *noun*
Etymology: Latin *raptus*

1. an expression or manifestation of ecstasy or passion

2. a: a state or experience of being carried away by overwhelming emotion b: a mystical experience in which the spirit is exalted to a knowledge of divine things

3. often capitalized : the final assumption of Christians into heaven during the end-time according to Christian theology synonym see *ECSTASY*

- rap·tur·ous 'rap-ch&-r&s, 'rap-shr&s/ *adjective*
- rap·tur·ous·ly *adverb*
- rap·tur·ous·ness *noun*

Within Webster's definition, we find recognition of the concept of the church's (Webster uses the term "Christians") "final assumption into heaven during the end time." If Webster defined the "Rapture" accurately as stated in "Christian theology," then this event is neither defined as secret, nor prior to an opportunity for a group of individuals to "believe as a result of a second chance" as specifically negated by definition of the term "final." Final disallows anything else!

Conducting both a biblical and a grammatical study of the word "rapture," two major and most critical revelations loom large and cause the heart to tremble.

1. If there is no "secret rapture," then believers are to know and understand every event preceding and accompanying the removal of the church, including the period known as "the time of trouble."

2. If the "final assumption" of Christians into heaven occurs during the "end time" according to Christian theology, the church must prayerfully read and, by the power and guidance of the

Holy Spirit, understand the book of Revelation. This is the only book remaining that, unlike any other, thoroughly depicts and explains end-time events.

*Is it too late? Do we have enough time to read, understand, prepare, go, and "having done all, to stand"* (Ephesians 6:13 (NIV)).

And at that time shall Michael stand up, the
great prince which standeth for the children
of thy people: and there shall be a time of
trouble, such as never was since there was a
nation even to that same time: and at that
time thy people shall be delivered, every one
that shall be found written in the book.

Daniel 12:1 (KJV)

The "Secret Rapture" theory is described as preceding a seven-year period known as "the time of Jacob's
trouble." It is believed the "gentile" church (Christian
believers) has been removed because by faith in Christ,
they are ready to live with him in heaven and thereby
avoid having to go through this final, terrible ordeal
reserved for the Jewish nation and individuals still
struggling with their faith. A search of God's Word for

clarification regarding "seven years of Jacob's trouble" resulted in verification that the Bible never once refers to this event. However, Jeremiah 30:7 prophetically references the end-time tribulation experienced by Israel and the church as witnessed by John and explained in Revelation chapters 7–13.

At this point it is very difficult to understand why or how Christians (those who follow Christ) came to accept a theory or presumed truth that does not come directly from God's Word. Willingness to accept a theory as truth because of the "source" when that source is other than the Word can have deadly and eternal consequences. What's even more tragic is to believe anything by faith in someone or something other than Christ and the Word. This practice leads to certain and eternal death. Are we, as professed followers of Christ believing in a "secret rapture, left behind" religion failing to "read and understand" prophecies regarding the "time of trouble" and the "investigative judgment" as required by Christ?

With new, yet unmistakable evidence challenging our beliefs, especially in these last and trying days, we are impressed with an urgency to accept and confirm every belief by two or three witnesses from the Word. His love for us, the work of the Spirit guiding us into all truth, will prevail if we test everything by the Word. We must remember that our Lord informs us that every secret will be made known.

> And he said unto them, Is a candle brought to be put under a bushel, or under a bed? and not to be set on a candlestick? For there is nothing hid, which shall not be manifested; neither was any thing kept secret, but that it should come abroad. If any man have ears to hear, let him hear.
>
> Mark 4:21–23 (NIV)

> This will take place on the day when God will judge men's secrets through Jesus Christ, as my gospel declares.
>
> Romans 2:16 (NIV)

> And Jesus said, For judgment I am come into this world, that they which see not might see; and that they which see might be made blind.
>
> John 9:39 (KJV)

But why dost thou judge thy brother? or why dost thou set at nought thy brother? for we shall all stand before the judgment seat of Christ.

Romans 14:10 (KJV)

For we must all appear before the judgment seat of Christ; that every one may receive the things done in his body, according to that he hath done, whether it be good or bad.

2 Corinthians 5:10 (KJV)

Herein is our love made perfect, that we may have boldness in the day of judgment: because as he is, so are we in this world.

1 John 4:17 (KJV)

He said in a loud voice, "Fear God and give him glory, because the hour of his judgment has come. Worship him who made the heavens, the earth, the sea and the springs of water."

Revelation 14:7 (NIV)

And unto the angel of the church of the
Laodiceans write; These things saith the
Amen, the faithful and true witness…

Revelation 3:14 (KJV)

In order that we would have evidence to believe his
Word and know the truth laid out for us in Matthew
24, Jesus states that "this generation" would witness
the events he foretold. An example of the historical
fulfillment and witness of certain Matthew 24 events
is supported by the writings of Paul. "And there stood
up one of them named Agabus, and signified by the
Spirit that there should be great dearth throughout all
the world: which came to pass in the days of Claudius
Caesar (Roman Empire)" (Acts 11:28, NIV).

As we study Revelation, we find additional instances of John's visions that qualify as a "witness" of Matthew 24 events:

> The revelation of Jesus Christ, which God gave him to show his servants what must soon take place. He made it known by sending his angel to his servant John, who testifies to everything he saw—that is, the word of God and the testimony of Jesus Christ. Blessed is the one who reads the words of this prophecy, and blessed are those who hear it and take to heart what is written in it, because the time is near.

Revelation 1:1–3 (NIV)

It is in Revelation then that we discover historical validation and confirmation of Matthew 24. Just as Christ had spoken prophetically by the Spirit, "I tell you the truth, this generation will certainly not pass away until all these things have happened" (Matthew 24:34, NIV), John, being present at the time Christ was speaking, qualifies as "this generation." Years after Christ's foretelling the events and manner of his return, John witnessed in vision the very events spoken of by Christ. It would be John, as an eyewitness to everything, who would record his witness of the time of trouble and related events yet to come upon the church and the earth prior to Christ's return. John "did not pass away" without seeing, and recording for us, the "end of the age" (Matthew 24:34, NIV). By this fulfillment of Christ's words, we are assured that Matthew 24, Daniel, Revelation, and the Bible still contains for us now, in this lifetime, specific guidance and instruction regarding actual, literal events leading up to and ushering in the second coming of Christ, including our (believers') whereabouts until then!

As we read to understand Revelation, we are admonished to prepare and act as though we believe our Lord is coming at any moment, in the twinkling of an eye. We are to accept and yield to the power of the Holy Spirit now, knowing we are being held accountable for our conduct and condition. We must look to last-day messages to guide us and establish our hearts in the truth. We must not believe that there is any portion of the Word to be ignored. Paul, led by the Spirit, admonished Christians, the body of Christ, to rely on the Word for life. "All Scripture is given by inspiration of God and is profitable for doctrine, for reproof, for correction, for instruction in righteousness: That the man of God may be perfect, thoroughly furnished unto all good works" (2 Timothy 3:16–17, KJV).

It is therefore quite wonderful to know that we can and must rely on the Word and only the Word for life and behavior. As we study events preceding and in preparation for the church's removal from this earth, we are not left to private or man's interpretation, conduct, or guidance regarding last-day events. What love the Father showers upon us! We are not left in the dark. We are not left to fear.

Revelation 1 to 12 introduces our Loving Savior as the Lamb slain for our redemption. In these chapters he provides guidance for our understanding and identifies the seven periods or phases of the church, following Christ's ascension to heaven following his resurrection. The messages to the churches contain evidence of the fulfillment of Matthew 24. In the period of the seventh church (our era), we are reminded of the pervasive, subtle, and destructive nature of sin within the body, among his children. We are also reminded of the terrible consequences and punishment awaiting the earth, falsehood, wickedness, and those who refuse to receive and be protected by the Truth. In chapters 13 and 14 of Revelation, just as in Daniel 2, 7, and 8, we are introduced to the concept and condition not much discussed or even considered today—the "Judgment"! (Alert—is the real "secret" the fact that the investigative gospel judgment of all created beings is going on now, not at or after death, and very few Christians know or understand that this judgment is taking place?). Understandably, as we read Christ's counsel to Laodicea (the "final assumptive" period in the history of the church), we realize why it is so very important to heed Christ's counsel and prescription necessary to stand before the "judgment seat of Christ" Romans 14:10.

I counsel you to buy from me gold refined in the fire, so you can become rich; and white clothes to wear, so you can cover your shameful nakedness; and salve to put on your eyes, so you can see. Those whom I love I rebuke and discipline. So be earnest, and repent.

Revelation 3:18–19 (NIV)

# 7

I tell you, now is the time of God's favor, now
is the day of salvation.

2 Corinthians 6:2 (NIV)

Read again carefully the instructions given us by
our Counselor in Revelation 3. Christ's message to
the churches and admonition to Laodicea makes it
clear that there is no other church after the Laodicean
church. No second chance. It is this "church," these
Christians, the "whosoever will" of today, both Jew
and Gentile, that must prepare; and whom are being
evaluated as to value, appearance, knowledge, and
conduct, now in this lifetime, before, not at the time
of nor after his second coming. There will be no second chances for Jew or Gentile after the period of the
seven churches. Now is the time of second chances
for all mankind. Ephesians teaches us that we are all

made one through the life, death, resurrection, and ascension of Christ.

> Therefore, remember that formerly you who are Gentiles by birth and called "uncircumcised" by those who call themselves "the circumcision" (that done in the body by the hands of men)—remember that at that time you were separate from Christ, excluded from citizenship in Israel and foreigners to the covenants of the promise, without hope and without God in the world. But now in Christ Jesus you who once were far away have been brought near through the blood of Christ. For he himself is our peace, who has made the two one and has destroyed the barrier, the dividing wall of hostility, by abolishing in his flesh the law with its commandments and regulations. His purpose was to create in himself one new man out of the two, thus making peace, and in this one body to reconcile both of them to God through the cross, by which he put to death their hostility. He came and preached peace to you who were

far away and peace to those who were near. For through him we both have access to the Father by one Spirit. Consequently, you are no longer foreigners and aliens, but fellow citizens with God's people and members of God's household, built on the foundation of the apostles and prophets, with Christ Jesus himself as the chief cornerstone. In him the whole building is joined together and rises to become a holy temple in the Lord. And in him you too are being built together to become a dwelling in which God lives by his Spirit.

Ephesians 2:11–22 (NIV)

Thus, it is clear why Christ instructs us that, for us, events prior to the removal of the church include an evaluation and an actual judgment including the final judgment of that "old serpent called the devil." No removal of the body without both Jew and Gentile. No time of trouble for purging or purifying and then accepting Christ for Jew or Gentile. No additional period of salvation for Jew or Gentile. No second chances after his return. "Now is the accepted time, today if you hear his voice harden not your hearts" (1 Corinthians 6:2 (KJV); Hebrews 3:15 (NIV)).

It makes sense then why Jesus commissioned us to preach this everlasting gospel to all, to every nation, kindred, tongue, and people. Understandably, our delay and failure to learn, believe, and share his truth, as a world church, and preach the everlasting gospel results in our Lord intervening. His gospel will go forth, even if it takes "babes" and "rocks" and "angels." John witnesses our Lord's remedy, in that Laodicea (ten virgins) is too consumed in lethargy to understand and believe the gospel, let alone "go ye therefore." He sees an angel flying in the midst of heaven proclaiming the everlasting gospel—a gospel of judgment and worship, a gospel of love.

Judgment must begin at the house of God...

I Peter 4:17 (KJV)

Before John ever wrote Revelation, before Paul became the apostle to the Gentiles, to ensure that "whosoever will" will know that "now is the accepted time," Christ and the Holy Spirit informed the world through Peter as to the only saving, sanctifying truth for all time:

> "But who do you say that I am?" Simon Peter answered and said, "You are the Christ, the Son of the living God." Jesus answered and said to him, "Blessed are you, Simon Bar-Jonah, for flesh and blood has not revealed this to you, but My Father who is in heaven. And I also say to you that you are Peter, and on this rock I will build My church, and the

> gates of Hades shall not prevail against it.
> And I will give you the keys of the kingdom
> of heaven, and whatever you bind on earth
> will be bound in heaven, and whatever you
> loose on earth will be loosed in heaven."

> Matthew 16:15–19 (NIV)

"Sidebar!" Know this, that "Rock," upon which the church is built, is the knowledge that Jesus is the Christ, the Son of the Living God!" To know and understand this declaration, to know who Christ is, this is life eternal, Christ, the Son of the Living God is that Rock! If you know who he is, you will believe and obey him! Back to the topic at hand, Peter, the apostle to the world church, wrote,

> "For the time is come that judgment must
> begin at the house of God: and if it first begin
> at us, what shall the end be of them that obey
> not the gospel of God?"

> 1 Peter 4:17, NIV

We don't like to consider, much less contemplate or ponder Christ's role as our "Judge." We don't especially care for any notion of "judgment." In many cases, honesty dictates that we admit that we only want Christ to save us in our sins. We want Christ to allow us to have salvation, eternal life, as we continue to sin. However, a search of Scripture regarding the work of Christ has, even prior to his birth, included the notion of his work in judgment necessary to eradicate sin. The Father's love for his children has always included instruction regarding the need for his own to receive his rules, "written upon the heart" for life and, in so doing, live.

> See, I will send my messenger, who will prepare the way before me. Then suddenly the Lord you are seeking will come to his temple; the messenger of the covenant, whom you desire, will come," says the LORD Almighty. But who can endure the day of his coming? Who can stand when he appears? For he will be like a refiner's fire or a launderer's soap. He will sit as a refiner and purifier of silver; he will purify the Levites and refine them like gold and silver. Then the LORD will have men

who will bring offerings in righteousness, and the offerings of Judah and Jerusalem will be acceptable to the LORD, as in days gone by, as in former years. "So I will come near to you for judgment. I will be quick to testify against sorcerers, adulterers and perjurers, against those who defraud laborers of their wages, who oppress the widows and the fatherless, and deprive aliens of justice, but do not fear me," says the LORD Almighty.

Malachi 3:1–5 (NIV)

See, I will send you the prophet Elijah before that great and dreadful day of the LORD comes. He will turn the hearts of the fathers to their children, and the hearts of the children to their fathers; or else I will come and strike the land with a curse.

Malachi 4:5–6 (NIV)

We know these texts refer to the work of John the Baptist and Christ at the time of his first advent as well as his work of judgment prior to his return. Acknowledging and understanding (faith) the work of judgment is critical then to understanding the magnitude of the Father's love and saving benefit of Christ's sacrifice. This faith prepares us to receive the seal of God and guarantees our place with him when he returns. It is the seal of God that prepares his own to endure and triumph through the judgment and the time of great tribulation.

> And after these things I saw four angels standing on the four corners of the earth, holding the four winds of the earth, that the wind should not blow on the earth, nor on the sea, nor on any tree. And I saw another angel ascending from the east, having the seal of the living God: and he cried with a loud voice to the four angels, to whom it was given to hurt the earth and the sea, Saying, Hurt not the earth, neither the sea, nor the trees, till we have sealed the servants of our God in their foreheads.
>
> Revelation 7:1–3 (KJV)

The court was seated, and the books were opened…

Daniel 7:10 (NIV)

How does the judgment work? How will we be judged? What happens when we are judged? What are the possible outcomes of the judgment? What can we do to achieve a favorable outcome or decision? Do we testify in our own behalf or plead the fifth?

> Then I saw another angel flying in midair, and he had the eternal gospel to proclaim to those who live on the earth—to every nation, tribe, language and people. He said in a loud voice, "Fear God and give him glory, because the hour of his judgment has come. Worship him who made the heavens, the earth, the sea

and the springs of water." A second angel followed and said, "Fallen! Fallen is Babylon the Great, which made all the nations drink the maddening wine of her adulteries." A third angel followed them and said in a loud voice: "If anyone worships the beast and his image and receives his mark on the forehead or on the hand, he, too, will drink of the wine of God's fury, which has been poured full strength into the cup of his wrath. He will be tormented with burning sulfur in the presence of the holy angels and of the Lamb. And the smoke of their torment rises for ever and ever. There is no rest day or night for those who worship the beast and his image, or for anyone who receives the mark of his name." This calls for patient endurance on the part of the saints who obey God's commandments and remain faithful to Jesus.

Revelation 14:6–12 (NIV)

Throughout Revelation we find Christ instructing his people, his (Laodicean) church, to worship him in obedience and faith because the "hour of God's judgment is come!" Interesting to note is that included in his call to worship him is an admonition to "come out of Babylon," this church that teaches lies and falsehoods, this church that does not worship the Creator of heaven and earth, the seas and fountains of water. He further admonishes that we must not worship the beast or receive his mark. Although many question how to avoid these destructive situations and influences, it is clear that Christ's remedy requires us to evaluate our condition, obey God's commandments by faith in his testimony, and be patient. "This calls for patient endurance on the part of the saints who obey God's commandments and remain faithful to Jesus" (Revelation 14:12, NIV).

When then will the judgment and the sealing occur for the Christian? Clearly God's Word lays out the time line for our judgment to begin and, more importantly, when judgment for his own, the church, and for that matter, when evil will end. First, we read in Daniel 7 (adhering to Christ's instruction to "let the reader understand" the prophetic testimony of Daniel):

As I looked, "thrones were set in place, and the Ancient of Days took his seat. His clothing was as white as snow; the hair of his head was white like wool. His throne was flaming with fire, and its wheels were all ablaze. A river of fire was flowing, coming out from before him. Thousands upon thousands attended him; ten thousand times ten thousand stood before him. The court was seated, and the books were opened..." "Then I wanted to know the true meaning of the fourth beast, which was different from all the others and most terrifying, with its iron teeth and bronze claws—the beast that crushed and devoured its victims and trampled underfoot whatever was left. I also wanted to know about the ten horns on its head and about the other horn that came up, before which three of them fell—the horn that looked more imposing than the others and that had eyes and a mouth that spoke boastfully. As I watched, this horn was waging war against the saints and defeating them, until the Ancient of Days came and pronounced judgment in favor of the saints of the Most

High, and the time came when they possessed the kingdom. "He gave me this explanation: 'The fourth beast is a fourth kingdom that will appear on earth. It will be different from all the other kingdoms and will devour the whole earth, trampling it down and crushing it. The ten horns are ten kings who will come from this kingdom. After them another king will arise, different from the earlier ones; he will subdue three kings. He will speak against the Most High and oppress his saints and try to change the set times and the laws. The saints will be handed over to him for a time, times and half a time.' But the court will sit, and his power will be taken away and completely destroyed forever. Then the sovereignty, power and greatness of the kingdoms under the whole heaven will be handed over to the saints, the people of the Most High. His kingdom will be an everlasting kingdom, and all rulers will worship and obey him.'" "He said to me, "It will take 2,300 evenings and mornings; then the sanctuary will be reconsecrated (cleansed)." "At that time Michael, the great prince who protects your people, will arise. There will be a time of distress such as has not happened from the beginning of nations until then. But at that time your people—everyone whose name is found written in the book—will be delivered. Multitudes who sleep in the dust of the earth will awake: some to everlasting life, others to shame and everlasting contempt. Those who are wise will shine like the brightness of the heavens, and those who lead many to righteousness, like the stars for ever and ever. But you, Daniel, close up and seal the words of the scroll until the time of the end. Many will go here and there to increase knowledge. "I heard, but I did not understand. So I asked, "My lord, what will the outcome of all this be?" He replied, "Go your way, Daniel, because the words are closed up and sealed until the time of the end. Many will be purified, made spotless and refined, but the wicked will continue to be wicked."

Daniel 7:9–10, 19–27; Daniel 8:14; Daniel 12:1–4, 8–10 (NIV)

The wicked, the unbelieving will fail to understand these great truths, but the wise, those with "Oil" in their lamps will, by his Spirit and grace, "understand." This is a promise! Just as light and understanding were given to Daniel in Babylon and Media Persia, just as John was given understanding while exiled to the isle of Patmos and was told to "seal not the sayings of this book," so then will understanding be given those earnestly seeking the truth to understand the "sayings of this book," to understand this time, and this event.

We all could have reason to fear the judgment and avoid dwelling upon the issue. Praise be to God, it is only by the Righteousness of Christ that anyone will be able to stand. As the Father evaluates each sin, judging by his perfect "law of liberty," He can only say: "You have neglected my word and have other gods before me, including husband, wife, children, grandchildren, job, sports, cars, money, sex, self. Guilty!" Christ's response, "*My blood*—Salvation. By *my spirit, my* child grows!—Sanctification."

"You have set up for yourselves graven images of houses, cars, clothes, television, DVDs, radios, MP3 players, cell phones, family, and other earthly things. You bow down before them and sacrifice to them. Guilty!" Christ's response, "*My blood*—Salvation. By *my spirit, my* child grows!—Sanctification."

"You have taken my name in vain with every 'Oh my Lord,' 'Oh my God,' 'Jesus Christ,' "Jesus H. Christ,' 'Godd***,' 'God,' 'Lord,' and other abusive uses of my name during every vile and degrading act of life. Guilty!" Christ's response, "*My blood*—Salvation. By *my spirit, my* child grows!—Sanctification."

"You refuse to remember the Sabbath day, my sacred and reverent time reserved for us, to keep it holy. You use it to shop, engage in work, sports, housekeeping, family obligations, secular entertainment, and selfish pleasures. When you do worship, you watch the clock anxious for dismissal, think self-centered, self-indulged thoughts, arrive late, leave early, and refuse to rest, worship, and relieve the burdens of the oppressed, fatherless, widows, and enslaved. Guilty!"

Christ's response, "*My blood*—Salvation. By *my spirit, my* child grows!—Sanctification."

"You neglect, profane, dishonor, abuse, criticize, hurt, and humiliate your parents and those I place in authority over you. Guilty!" Christ's response, "*My blood*—Salvation. By *my spirit, my* child grows!—Sanctification."

"You destroy life by your words and lust after death, violence, and destruction with your eyes, hearts, and minds in music, video, and interests. Guilty!" Christ's response, "*My blood*—Salvation. By *my spirit, my* child grows!—Sanctification."

"You lust for, divorce, and abandon one another in my church and in your homes. You excuse every act of fornication, adultery, and every perversion. Guilty!" Christ's response, "*My blood*—Salvation. By *my spirit my* child grows!—Sanctification."

"You take what does not belong to you, including my tithe and offerings. Guilty!" Christ's response, "*My blood*—Salvation. By *my spirit my* child grows!—Sanctification."

"You tell lies and manipulate the truth as though you neither know me nor trust me. Guilty!" Christ's response, "*My blood!*—Salvation. By *my spirit my* child grows!—Sanctification."

"You do all this because you have faith in the things around you, things belonging to others, as though belonging to someone else gives it value and power for you. Guilty!" Christ's response, "*My blood*—Salvation. By *my spirit my* child grows!—Sanctification."

How shall we stand in the presence of a Holy God when our name is called? Is there any hope for us? Is there any way that our names will remain in the Lamb's Book of Life?

> For Christ did not enter a man-made sanctuary that was only a copy of the true one; he entered heaven itself, now to appear for us in God's presence. Nor did he enter heaven to offer himself again and again, the way the high priest enters the Most Holy Place every year with blood that is not his own. Then Christ would have had to suffer many times since the creation of the world. But now he has appeared once for all at the end of the ages to do away with sin by the sacrifice of

himself. Just as man is destined to die once, and after that to face judgment, so Christ was sacrificed once to take away the sins of many people; and he will appear a second time, not to bear sin, but to bring salvation to those who are waiting for him. Let us then approach the throne of grace with confidence, so that we may receive mercy and find grace to help us in our time of need. How much more, then, will the blood of Christ, who through the eternal Spirit offered himself unblemished to God, cleanse our consciences from acts that lead to death, so that we may serve the living God!

Hebrews 9:24–28; 4:16; 9:14 (NIV)

This calls for patient endurance on the part of the saints who obey God's commandments and remain faithful to Jesus.

Revelation 14:12 (NIV)

"This is the covenant I will make with the house of Israel after that time," declares the LORD. "I will put my law in their minds and write it on their hearts. I will be their God, and they will be my people."

Jeremiah 31:33 (NIV)

This is the covenant I will make with the house of Israel after that time, declares the Lord. I will put my laws in their minds and write them on their hearts. I will be their God, and they will be my people.

Hebrews 8:10

For there is no respect of persons with God. For as many as have sinned without law shall also perish without law: and as many as have sinned in the law shall be judged by the law; (For not the hearers of the law are just before God, but the doers of the law shall be justified. For when the Gentiles, which have not the law, do by nature the things contained in the law, these, having not the law, are a law unto themselves: Which shew the work of the law written in their hearts, their conscience also bearing witness…

Romans 2:11–15 (KJV)

Shall I crucify your King? The chief priests answered, 'We have no king but Caesar.'

John 19:15 (KJV)

We know that during the period of the "little horn" (the fourth (iron) kingdom identified in Daniel 2 and 7), the judgment begins. We must now make certain to identify this "iron kingdom" and learn when and where it begins (remembering that this kingdom does not end until Christ's return). Let us quickly review the four kingdoms described throughout the book of Daniel. Do you remember King Nebuchadnezzar's dream?

> This is the dream. Now we will tell the interpretation of it before the king. You, O king, are a king of kings. For the God of heaven has given you a kingdom, power, strength, and glory; and wherever the children of men dwell,

or the beasts of the field and the birds of the heaven, he has given them into your hand, and has made you ruler over them all—you are this head of gold. But after you shall arise another kingdom inferior to yours; then another, a third kingdom of bronze, which shall rule over all the earth. And the fourth kingdom shall be as strong as iron, inasmuch as iron breaks in pieces and shatters everything; and like iron that crushes, that kingdom will break in pieces and crush all the others.

Daniel 2:36–40 (NIV)

Babylon is the first beast (kingdom). Daniel 8 provides the names of the next two beasts (kingdoms) mentioned in Daniel's explanation of King Nebuchadnezzar's dream. Explaining the details of his vision, Daniel writes, "I looked up, and there before me was a ram with two horns standing beside the canal, and the horns were long. One of the horns (Persia) was longer than the other (Media) but grew up later" (Daniel 8:3 NIV)). "The two horned ram which you saw represents the kings of Media and Persia" (Daniel 8:20 (NIV)). (Whom of us does not remember the story of the young maiden Esther, anointed by God to deliver his people from death when she was chosen as Queen by the Persian King Ahasuerus?)

> Suddenly a goat (Greece) with a prominent horn (Alexander) between his eyes came from the west, crossing the whole earth without touching the ground. He came toward the two-horned ram I had seen standing beside the canal and charged at him in great rage. I saw him attack the ram furiously, striking the ram and shattering his two horns. The ram was powerless to stand against him; the goat knocked him to the ground and trampled on him, and none could rescue the ram from his power. The goat became very great, but at the height of his power his large horn was broken off, and in its place four prominent horns [Cassander, Lysimachus, Seleucus I Nicator, Ptolemy I.][1] grew up toward the four winds of heaven."

Daniel 8:5–8 (NIV)

Again, just as the first beast is named, the second and third beasts are named in God's Word. The dual kingdoms of Media-Persia and the kingdom of Greece led first by Alexander the Great, as well as its subsequent division among four minor leaders following his death, are mentioned. These two kingdoms follow the first kingdom (Babylon) to take God's chosen people into captivity. The fourth kingdom, though not named, is described as the iron kingdom and exists during the time of Christ as detailed in Daniel.

> 'Those great beasts, which are four, are four kings which arise out of the earth. But the saints of the Most High shall receive the kingdom, and possess the kingdom forever, even forever and ever.' "Then I wished to know the truth about the fourth beast, which was different from all the others, exceedingly dreadful, with its teeth of iron and its nails of bronze, which devoured, broke in pieces, and trampled the residue with its feet; and the ten horns that were on its head, and the other horn which came up, before which three fell, namely, that horn which had eyes and a mouth which spoke pompous words, whose

appearance was greater than his fellows. "I was watching; and the same horn was making war against the saints, and prevailing against them, until the Ancient of Days came, and a judgment was made in favor of the saints of the Most High, and the time came for the saints to possess the kingdom.

"Thus he said:
'The fourth beast shall be
A fourth kingdom on earth,
Which shall be different from all other kingdoms,
And shall devour the whole earth,
Trample it and break it in pieces.
The ten horns are ten kings
Who shall arise from this kingdom.
And another shall rise after them;
He shall be different from the first ones,
And shall subdue three kings.
He shall speak pompous words against the Most High,
Shall persecute the saints of the Most High,
And shall intend to change times and law.

Then the saints shall be given into his hand
For a time and times and half a time.
26 ' But the court shall be seated,
And they shall take away his dominion,
To consume and destroy it forever.

Daniel 7:17–26 (NKJV), emphasis added

That fourth beast, destroying and following Greece, was the Roman Empire. We know Rome to have persecuted the saints, including our Lord, and it is during the era of Rome as a global power that the judgment begins (read the entire book of Daniel, paying close attention to chapters 2, 7 through 10, and 12).

It is important for each person to know that he will be judged. It is even more important to know when one will be judged. The fulfillment of our goals and desires (earthly and eternal) are tied to the outcome of each one's hearing. Two questions must be answered: "What do I want for my life now, and how do I want to spend eternity?" No matter what a person's belief system, our mortality and our inability to control what may happen next in no way diminishes the reality that the outcome to these questions is the result of the choices we make now in this lifetime.

> Then I saw another angel flying in midair, and he had the eternal gospel to proclaim to those who live on the earth—to every nation, tribe, language and people. He said in a loud voice, "Fear God and give him glory, because the hour of his judgment has come. Worship him who made the heavens, the earth, the sea and the springs of water. A second angel followed and said, "Fallen! Fallen is Babylon the Great, which made all the nations drink the maddening wine of her adulteries." A third angel followed them and said in a loud voice: "If anyone worships the beast and his image and receives his mark on the forehead or on the hand, he, too, will drink of the wine of God's fury, which has been poured full strength into the cup of his wrath. He will be tormented with burning sulfur in the presence of the holy angels and of the Lamb. And the smoke of their torment rises for ever and ever. There is no rest day or night for those

who worship the beast and his image, or for anyone who receives the mark of his name." This calls for patient endurance on the part of the saints who obey God's commandments and remain faithful to Jesus.

Revelation 14:6–12 (NIV)

With the knowledge that we are being judged regarding our obedience to the Commandments of God and faithfulness to Jesus, it is wonderful and reassuring to remember that if we have fallen, we have an Advocate, Intercessor, and High Priest who is able to keep us.

My little children, these things write I unto you, that ye sin not. And if any man sin, we have an advocate with the Father, Jesus Christ the righteous.

John 2:1 (NIV)

Who is he that condemns? Christ Jesus, who died—more than that, who was raised to life—is at the right hand of God and is also interceding for us.

Romans 8:34 (NIV)

The point here is this, "We do have such a high priest, who sat down at the right hand of the throne of the Majesty in heaven, and who serves in the sanctuary, the true tabernacle set up by the Lord, not by man" (Hebrews 8:1–2, NIV). Let each pray to him now that we, by the power of the Holy Spirit, yield our hearts, minds, and lives to the Spirit's work, will, and converting power. Let each of us pray for and allow the Spirit to write God's commandments on our hearts, receive by faith the testimony of Jesus, and be sealed for our Lord today.

> "Behold, what manner of love the Father hath bestowed upon us…"
>
> 1 John 3:1 (KJV)

# 11

Lightning…Trumpets…the Heavenly
Host…and the King of Kings…

Matthew 24: 27, 31; Luke 17:24;
1 Corinthians 15:52

Every eye shall see him…

Revelation 1:7

## Where's the Secret?

Now that we understand and have been fore-
warned that there is a judgment taking place in heaven
before our Lord's return, and that it is going on now,
we understand our need for the sanctifying work of
the Holy Spirit. It is only through his ministry on our
behalf and his indwelling that we can receive the seal
of God and the righteousness of Christ to be able to
stand. But more than this, it also becomes even more

significant that we understand the final outcome of the judgment. Daniel and Revelation tell us the end of the judgment will result in the coming of our Lord to receive his own. It is wonderful to be able to rely on the Word, not man's theories and doctrines, to guide us in our study of events accompanying the removal of the church—Christ's "elect" at his coming.

> "So if anyone tells you, 'There he is, out in the desert,' do not go out; or, 'Here he is, in the inner rooms,' do not believe it. For as lightning that comes from the east is visible even in the west, so will be the coming of the Son of Man. Wherever there is a carcass, there the vultures will gather. At that time the sign of the Son of Man will appear in the sky, and all the nations of the earth will mourn. They will see the Son of Man coming on the clouds of the sky, with power and great glory. And he will send his angels with a loud trumpet call, and they will gather his elect from the four winds, from one end of the heavens to the other."

"I declare to you, brothers, that flesh and blood cannot inherit the kingdom of God, nor does the perishable inherit the imperishable. Listen, I tell you a mystery: We will not all sleep, but we will all be changed—in a flash, in the twinkling of an eye, at the last trumpet. For the trumpet will sound, the dead will be raised imperishable, and we will be changed. For the perishable must clothe itself with the imperishable, and the mortal with immortality. When the perishable has been clothed with the imperishable, and the mortal with immortality, then the saying that is written will come true: "Death has been swallowed up in victory." "Where, O death, is your victory? Where, O death, is your sting?" The sting of death is sin, and the power of sin is the law. But thanks be to God! He gives us the victory through our Lord Jesus Christ. Therefore, my dear brothers, stand firm. Let nothing move you. Always give yourselves fully to the work of the Lord, because you know that your labor in the Lord is not in vain. "Brothers, we do not want you to be ignorant about those who fall asleep, or to grieve like the rest of men, who have no hope. We believe that Jesus died and rose again and so we believe that God will bring with Jesus those who have fallen asleep in him. According to the Lord's own word, we tell you that we who are still alive, who are left till the coming of the Lord, will certainly not precede those who have fallen asleep. For the Lord himself will come down from heaven, with a loud command, with the voice of the archangel and with the trumpet call of God, and the dead in Christ will rise first. After that, we who are still alive and are left will be caught up together with them in the clouds to meet the Lord in the air. And so we will be with the Lord forever. Therefore encourage each other with these words."

Matthew 24:26–28, 30–31; 1 Corinthians 15:50–57; 1 Thessalonians 4:13–18 (NIV)

"I looked, and there before me was a white cloud, and seated on the cloud was one "like a son of man" with a crown of gold on his head and a sharp sickle in his hand. Then another angel came out of the temple and called in a loud voice to him who was sitting on the cloud, "Take your sickle and reap, because the time to reap has come, for the harvest of the earth is ripe." So he who was seated on the cloud swung his sickle over the earth, and the earth was harvested.

Revelation 14:14–16 (NIV)

Do not let your hearts be troubled. Trust in God; trust also in me. In my Father's house are many rooms; if it were not so, I would have told you. I am going there to prepare a place for you. And if I go and prepare a place for you, I will come back and take you to be with me that you also may be where I am.

John 4:1–3 (NIV)

Behold, he cometh with clouds; and every eye shall see him, and they also which pierced him: and all kindreds of the earth shall wail because of him. Even so, Amen.

Revelation 1:7 (KJV)

And for this cause God shall send them strong delusion, that they should believe a lie…

2 Thessalonians 2:11 (NIV)

Unlike Daniel, who was told, "But thou, O Daniel, shut up the words, and seal the book, even to the time of the end: many shall run to and fro, and knowledge shall be increased" (Daniel 12:4, KJV), John is instructed, "And he saith unto me, Seal not the sayings of the prophecy of this book: for the time is at hand" (Revelation 22:10, KJV).

Undoubtedly John must have recalled Christ's own instructions found in Matthew 24 as he received the angelic admonition "seal not" or do not "withhold" the information contained in the book of Revelation.

And this gospel of the kingdom shall be preached in all the world for a witness unto all nations; and then shall the end come. When ye therefore shall see the abomination of desolation, spoken of by Daniel the prophet, stand in the holy place, (whoso readeth, let him understand:)...

Matthew 24:14–15 (KJV)

It appears that the true secret is that the "secret rapture" theory is preventing believers from studying, reading, and understanding end-time prophecy and events. There is an eternally destructive outcome for the belief in a "snatching away" of the church, and a second chance to accept Christ during a terrible "time of trouble." This deception is leading much of the Christian world church to refuse to read the book of Revelation. Many are willingly ignorant of the period of the heavenly judgment and that it is going on now. Professed followers of Christ prefer to rely on the teaching of men rather than God and are therefore failing to prepare, just as the five foolish virgins, for the bridegroom's coming.

A global rejection of the Word and failure to prepare for the coming of our Lord is just as depicted and foretold by Paul,

> Concerning the coming of our Lord Jesus Christ and our being gathered to him, we ask you, brothers, not to become easily unsettled or alarmed by some prophecy, report or letter supposed to have come from us, saying that the day of the Lord has already come. Don't let anyone deceive you in any way, for (that day will not come) until the rebellion occurs and the man of lawlessness is revealed, the man doomed to destruction. He will oppose and will exalt himself over everything that is called God or is worshiped, so that he sets himself up in God's temple, proclaiming himself to be God. Don't you remember that when I was with you I used to tell you these things? And now you know what is holding him back, so that he may be revealed at the proper time. For the secret power of lawlessness is already at work; but the one who now holds it back will continue to do so till he is

taken out of the way. And then the lawless one will be revealed, whom the Lord Jesus will overthrow with the breath of his mouth and destroy by the splendor of his coming. The coming of the lawless one will be in accordance with the work of Satan displayed in all kinds of counterfeit miracles, signs and wonders, and in every sort of evil that deceives those who are perishing. They perish because they refused to love the truth and so be saved. For this reason God sends them a powerful delusion so that they will believe the lie and so that all will be condemned who have not believed the truth but have delighted in wickedness.

But we ought always to thank God for you, brothers loved by the Lord, because from the beginning God chose you to be saved through the sanctifying work of the Spirit and through belief in the truth. He called you to this through our gospel, that you might share in the glory of our Lord Jesus Christ. So then, brothers, stand firm and hold to the teachings we passed on to you, whether by word of mouth or by letter. May our Lord Jesus Christ himself and God our Father, who loved us and by his grace gave us eternal encouragement and good hope, encourage your hearts and strengthen you in every good deed and word."

2 Thessalonians 2:1–16 (NIV)

The masses, by accepting to believe the lie, are steeped in the delusion that the church will be gone during the time of the fulfillment of the prophecy and terrible tribulation described in Revelation; and thereby do not read, study, and understand this book. How can we be prepared to endure what lies ahead if we don't know or, worse yet, choose not to know what is coming upon the earth because we rather "believe a lie"? (2 Thessalonians 2:11, KJV) Whatever we chose to do, or not do, whatever, or whoever we may blame for what we do or do not do, believe, or say, the Word of God is true, the book is open for Holy Spirit-led study and understanding! We are without excuse!

What dreadful consequences await those who fail to receive the truth, whosoever rejects the Word of God and fails to allow the Holy Spirit to write his commandments upon their heart.

> And it was commanded them that they should not hurt the grass of the earth, neither any green thing, neither any tree; but only those men which have not the seal of God in their foreheads.
>
> Revelation 9:4 (KJV)

And he saith unto me, Seal not the sayings
of the prophecy of this book: for the time is
at hand.

Revelation 22:10 (KJV)

We now must realize that Revelation reveals and
explains what John, through Christ as well as the
patriarchs and prophets through the ages, saw—the
wondrous events taking place in heaven prior to and
after the Christians' arrival there. If we ask for Holy
Spirit guidance, we can read and understand the book
of Revelation, every prophetic event and glory. Just
imagine, we have been empowered, I dare say, we
have been commanded by our Lord to see by faith
the true vision of the church at home with Christ, as
shown John.

After the vision concerning the beast, his image, and mark, John writes,

> And I saw another angel ascending from the east, having the seal of the living God: and he cried with a loud voice to the four angels, to whom it was given to hurt the earth and the sea, Saying, Hurt not the earth, neither the sea, nor the trees, till we have sealed the servants of our God in their foreheads. And I heard the number of them which were sealed: and there were sealed a hundred and forty four thousand of all the tribes of the children of Israel. Then I looked, and there before me was the Lamb, standing on Mount Zion, and with him 144,000 who had his name and his Father's name written on their foreheads. And I heard a sound from heaven like the roar of rushing waters and like a loud peal of thunder. The sound I heard was like that of harpists playing their harps. And they sang a new song before the throne and before the four living creatures and the elders. No one could learn the song except the 144,000 who

had been redeemed from the earth. These are those who did not defile themselves with women, for they kept themselves pure. They follow the Lamb wherever he goes. They were purchased from among men and offered as firstfruits to God and the Lamb. No lie was found in their mouths; they are blameless.

Revelation 7:2–4; Revelation 14:1–5 (KJV)

This elite group is the first view of the redeemed saints in heaven gathered from the twelve tribes of Israel as witnessed by John. It is important to note that this vision follows the period of the "mark of the beast" and an intense period of terrible oppression and trial for the saints.

Then I saw another beast, coming out of the earth. He had two horns like a lamb, but he spoke like a dragon. He exercised all the authority of the first beast on his behalf, and made the earth and its inhabitants worship the first beast, whose fatal wound had been healed. And he performed great and miraculous signs, even causing fire to come down from heaven to earth in full view of men. Because of the signs he was given power to do on behalf of the first beast, he deceived the inhabitants of the earth. He ordered them to set up an image in honor of the beast who was wounded by the sword and yet lived. He was given power to give breath to the image of the first beast, so that it could speak and cause all who refused to worship the image to be killed. He also forced everyone, small and great, rich and poor, free and slave, to receive a mark on his right hand or on his forehead, so that no one could buy or sell unless he had the mark, which is the name of the beast or the number of his name. This calls for wisdom. If anyone has insight, let him calculate the number of the beast, for it is man's number. His number is 666.

Revelation 13:11–18 (NIV)

Once again, we must acknowledge that even in the case of the 144,000, these saints, redeemed from the earth, who follow the Lamb "wherever he goes," are seen in heaven only after the church goes through a period of dreadful persecution:

> After this I beheld, and, lo, a great multitude, which no man could number, of all nations, and kindreds, and people, and tongues, stood before the throne, and before the Lamb, clothed with white robes, and palms in their hands; And cried with a loud voice, saying, Salvation to our God which sitteth upon the throne, and unto the Lamb. And all the angels stood round about the throne, and about the elders and the four beasts, and fell before the throne on their faces, and worshiped God, Saying, Amen: Blessing, and glory, and wisdom and thanksgiving, and honor and power, and might, be unto our God forever and ever. Amen. And one of the elders answered, saying unto me, What are these which are arrayed in white robes? and whence came they? And I said unto him, Sir, thou knowest. And he said to me, These are they which came out of great tribulation, and have washed their robes, and made them white in the blood of the Lamb.

Therefore are they before the throne of God, and serve him day and night in his temple: and he that sitteth on the throne shall dwell among them. They shall hunger no more, neither thirst any more; neither shall the sun light on them, nor any heat. For the Lamb which is in the midst of the throne shall feed them, and shall lead them unto living fountains of waters: and God shall wipe away all tears from their eyes.

Revelation 7:9–17 (KJV)

It is only after the 144,000 from the twelve tribes of Israel are seen in heaven, following their deliverance from great persecution, that John sees a number that no man can number (redeemed Christians in heaven) wearing white robes, having endured and come out of great tribulation by the blood of the lamb. *Not prior to*!

Finally, following several chapters describing the acts of rebellion and apostasy by the beast, false prophet, and false church, and the nature and manner of their punishment (as well as the destruction of those whose names are not found written in the Lamb's Book of Life), we are shown the redemption of the body of Christ, the saints redeemed from the earth, in heaven with Christ. *Hallelujah!*

> After this I heard what sounded like the roar of a great multitude in heaven shouting: "Hallelujah! Salvation and glory and power belong to our God, for true and just are his judgments. He has condemned the great prostitute who corrupted the earth by her adulteries. He has avenged on her the blood of his servants." And again they shouted: "Hallelujah! The smoke from her goes up for ever and ever." The twenty-four elders and the four living creatures fell down and worshiped God, who was seated on the throne. And they cried: "Amen, Hallelujah!" Then a voice came from the throne, saying: "Praise our God, all you his servants, you who fear him, both small and great!" Then I heard what sounded like a great multitude, like the roar of rushing waters and like loud peals of thunder, shouting: "Hallelujah! For our Lord

God Almighty reigns. Let us rejoice and be glad and give him glory! For the wedding of the Lamb has come, and his bride has made herself ready. Fine linen, bright and clean, was given her to wear." [Fine linen stands for the righteous acts of the saints]. Then the angel said to me, "Write: 'Blessed are those who are invited to the wedding supper of the Lamb!' "And he added, "These are the true words of God."

Revelation 19:1–9 (NIV)

I was young and now I am old, yet I have never seen the righteous forsaken or their children begging bread.

Psalm 37:25 (KJV)

Much will take place immediately prior to and at the time of the coming of our Lord. Events terrible for the unbelieving await them. Most profound and disregarded by much of the world church, regardless as to specific denomination, are the removal of the Holy Spirit and the releasing of the four angels holding back the winds of destruction. God has told us from the very beginning that man will not always have the pleading, power, and presence of the Spirit, "And the LORD said, My Spirit shall not always strive with man, for that he also is flesh" (Genesis 6:3, KJV). Jesus, suffering separation from the Father and Holy Spirit, was our example of the dreadful agony experienced in separation. Even though his perfect walk with the Father by the power of the anointing Spirit demonstrated the sinless life of one who had the law of the Lord written upon his heart, he still had to endure that period of separation, as will those of us who will be alive and remain till the coming of our Lord. "My God, My God, why hast thou forsaken me?" (Matthew 27:46, KJV)

We find early in the book of Revelation John witnessing the sealing of the saints prior to the release of the angels prepared to bring global destruction upon those who fail to have the seal of God.

> And I saw another angel ascending from the east, having the seal of the living God: and he cried with a loud voice to the four angels, to whom it was given to hurt the earth and the sea, Saying, Hurt not the earth, neither the sea, nor the trees, till we have sealed the servants of our God in their foreheads.
>
> Revelation 7:2–3 (NIV)

After reading the entire chapter, as well as Revelation 13 and 14, it is clear that Israel (144,000) and Gentiles (number no man could number), in other words, Christ's body, is redeemed from the earth out of great tribulation and persecution. Once again, not prior to it! This is no secret!

The truth, relative to the "sealing" work of the Holy Spirit prior to the Lord's return, is also substantiated by Paul, apostle to the Gentiles and the world church. "Who hath also sealed us, and given the earnest of the Spirit in our hearts" (2 Corinthians, 1:22 NIV). "And grieve not the Holy Spirit of God, whereby ye are sealed unto the day of redemption" (Ephesians 4:30, NIV). It is therefore the "sealing," the life-changing work of the Holy Spirit, which sustains the servants and saints of God during the time of tribulation and persecution. A day will come when the Spirit's work will be finished.

> He that is unjust, let him be unjust still and
> he that is filthy, let him be filthy still: and he
> that is righteous, let him be righteous still:
> and he that is holy, let him be holy still.

> Revelation 22:11 (KJV)

And the LORD said, My Spirit shall not always strive with man, for that he also is flesh.

Genesis 6:3 (KJV)

Should we then fear? Absolutely not! No, not at all. Love does not allow it! We are not uninformed. We are not unaware of what is to come upon the earth.

As it was in the days of Noah, so it will be at the coming of the Son of Man. For in the days before the flood, people were eating and drinking, marrying and giving in marriage, up to the day Noah entered the ark; and they knew nothing about what would happen until the flood came and took them all away. That is how it will be at the coming of the Son of Man. Two men will be in the field; one will be taken and the other left. Two women will be grinding with a hand mill; one will be taken and the other left. Therefore keep watch, because you do not know on what day your Lord will come. But understand this: If the owner of the house had known at what time of night the thief was coming, he would have kept watch and would not have let his house be broken into. So you also must be ready, because the Son of Man will come at an hour when you do not expect him.

Matthew 24:37–44 (NIV)

Our Lord always protects his children. We have witnessed how completely God's people (Israel of old) were spared the plagues and tragedy that befell Egypt as a result of Pharaoh's stubborn and rebellious will. He was told and shown truth but refused to surrender.

And all the Egyptians dug along the Nile to get drinking water, because they could not drink the water of the river. Then Pharaoh summoned Moses and Aaron and said, "Pray to the LORD to take the frogs away from me and my people...The houses of the Egyptians will be full of flies, and even the ground where they are. But on that day I will deal differently with the land of Goshen, where my people live; no swarms of flies will be there, so that you will know that I, the LORD, am in this land. I will make a distinction between my people and your people. This miraculous sign will occur tomorrow. The hand of the LORD will bring a terrible plague on your livestock in the field—on your horses and donkeys and camels and on your cattle and sheep and goats. But the LORD will make a distinction between the livestock of Israel and that of Egypt, so that no animal belonging to the Israelites will die. The LORD set a time and said, "Tomorrow the LORD will do this in the land." And the next day the LORD did it: All the livestock of the Egyptians died, but not one animal belonging to the Israelites died. The magicians could not stand before Moses because of the boils that were on them and on all the Egyptians. Throughout Egypt hail struck everything in the fields—both men and animals; it beat down everything growing in the fields and stripped every tree. The only place it did not hail was the land of Goshen, where the Israelites were. So Moses stretched out his hand toward the sky, and total darkness covered all Egypt for three days. No one could see anyone else or leave his place for three days. Yet all the Israelites had light in the places where they lived."

Exodus 7:24; 8:7, 21–23; 9:3–6, 11, 25–26; 10:22–23 (NIV)

Is not this our Lord's promise to those who love him and obey him?

Because thou hast made the LORD, which is my refuge, even the most High, thy habitation; there shall no evil befall thee, neither shall any plague come nigh thy dwelling. For he shall give his angels charge over thee, to keep thee in all thy ways.

Psalm 91:9–11 (KJV)

*Boundless love! We need only remember "whose" we are and what manner of Christian we ought to be.*

Who then is the faithful and wise servant, whom the master has put in charge of the servants in his household to give them their food at the proper time? It will be good for that servant whose master finds him doing so when he returns. I tell you the truth, he will put him in charge of all his possessions. But suppose that servant is wicked and says to himself, 'My master is staying away a long time,' and he then begins to beat his fellow servants and to eat and drink with drunkards. The master of that servant will come on a day when he does not expect him and at an hour he is not aware of. He will cut him to pieces and assign him a place with the hypocrites, where there will be weeping and gnashing of teeth.

Matthew 24:45–51 (NIV)

When the Holy Spirit is removed from the earth, and man goes through the terrible tribulation yet to come, we must remember what the Lord has promised; we must remember His Word. Although the world church and church leaders have failed to proclaim the everlasting gospel of judgment and worship, the "secret" is no longer a mystery. Remember, the

Lord will protect and pass over the dwellings of those who love and obey him.

> Then Moses summoned all the elders of Israel and said to them, "Go at once and select the animals for your families and slaughter the Passover lamb. Take a bunch of hyssop, dip it into the blood in the basin and put some of the blood on the top and on both sides of the doorframe. Not one of you shall go out the door of his house until morning. When the LORD goes through the land to strike down the Egyptians, he will see the blood on the top and sides of the doorframe and will pass over that doorway, and he will not permit the destroyer to enter your houses and strike you down.
>
> Exodus 12:21–23 (NIV)

After this, Jesus knowing that all things were now accomplished, that the Scripture might be fulfilled, saith, I thirst. Now there was set a vessel full of vinegar: and they filled a sponge with vinegar, and put it upon hyssop, and put it to his mouth. When Jesus therefore had received the vinegar, he said, It is finished: and he bowed his head, and gave up the ghost…But when they came to Jesus, and saw that he was dead already, they broke not his legs: But one of the soldiers with a spear pierced his side, and forthwith came there out blood and water. And he that saw it bare record, and his record is true: and he knoweth that he saith true, that ye might believe. For these things were done, that the Scripture should be fulfilled…

John 19:28–30, 33–36 (KJV)

Jesus has indeed become our *passover*! Love facing love interceding for us.

# Epilogue

Be ye also ready…Knowing these things
what manner of person ought ye to be?

Matthew 24:44; 2 Peter 3:11 (KJV)

"Unexpected" is not synonymous with secret.

All who will stand before the judgment seat of
Christ must by his Spirit have the commandments of
God and the faith of Jesus written upon their heart now,
so as to stand when the Spirit of God ceases to strive
with "man." How is this possible for sinners saved by
grace? Accept Jesus Christ as your personal Lord and
receive his robe of righteousness. Allow the Holy Spirit
through sanctifying trials to create in you a heart of
"gold." Receive from that same Spirit the "white rai-

ment" that you may be clothed in the robe of Christ's righteousness. Let him anoint your spiritual vision with the "eye salve" of his Word. You will be empowered by the blood of Jesus Christ to live as the Father requires, as justice demands, and as your own heart truly desires.

Like Elizabeth and Zechariah, "both of them were upright in the sight of God, observing all the Lord's commandments and regulations blamelessly" (Luke 1:6, NIV), you who are living in the last days will serve the Father by the power of the Holy Spirit given to you when you ask Jesus, your Savior. You will have a Spirit-perfected (sealed) nature able to stand in that "great day" without a mediator. Then will be demonstrated in each one the words of Christ, "Be ye therefore perfect even as your Father which is in heaven is perfect" (Matthew 5:28, KJV).

"Here are they that keep the commandments of God and the faith of Jesus" (Revelation 14:12, NIV)).

> Then the dragon was enraged at the woman and went off to make war against the rest of her offspring—those who obey God's commandments and hold to the testimony of

Jesus. This calls for patient endurance on the part of the saints who obey God's commandments and remain faithful to Jesus.

Revelation 12:17; 14:12 (NIV)

And he that keepeth his commandments dwelleth in him, and he in him. And hereby we know that he abideth in us, by the Spirit which he hath given us.

1 John 3:24 (KJV)

This message of love, the everlasting gospel, is for all—whosoever. Remember, you are not to believe anything unless supported in and by God's Word, by two or three witnesses. Test everything by this biblical standard.

Any Christian who has studied the nature of science (commonly referred to as the scientific method) has learned to utilize five principles for arriving at a conclusion based upon repeated experimentation and testable evidence. By the "Way, the Truth, and the Life," you can test and know his plan for your life.

"Let us hear the conclusion of the whole matter."

Ecclesiastes 12:13 (KJV)

*Observation*
*Define the Problem*
Many believers accept a theory that the church is awaiting a secret removal from the earth after which there will be a devastating time of trouble at which time some, including the converts from the Jewish nation, will be saved. Does God's Word teach or support this concept?

*Research*
God's Word teaches that believers will be removed from the earth by his angels at his coming and out of a time of persecution unlike any before, at the end of the investigative judgment. "These were more noble than those in Thessalonica, in that they received the word with all readiness of mind, and searched the scriptures daily, whether those things were so" (Acts 17:11, KJV).

At that time Michael, the great prince who protects your people, will arise. There will be a time of distress such as has not happened from the beginning of nations until then. But at that time your people—everyone whose name is found written in the book—will be delivered. Multitudes who sleep in the dust of the earth will awake: some to everlasting life, others to shame and everlasting contempt. Those who are wise will shine like the brightness of the heavens, and those who lead many to righteousness, like the stars for ever and ever.

Daniel 12:1–3 (KJV)

*Hypothesis*

Christ and the Word do not teach that there is a "secret rapture" removal of the church prior to our Lord's return. No second chances for Jew or Gentile. Now is the accepted time. Now is the time of God's judgment of this world.

*Experiment*

*Materials*

Word of God, Testimony of Jesus Christ, Holy Spirit, and Prayer

*Procedure*

> In the mouth of two or three witnesses every word may be established.
>
> Matthew 18:16 (KJV)

And I saw another angel fly in the midst of heaven, having the everlasting gospel to preach unto them that dwell on the earth, and to every nation, and kindred, and tongue, and people, Saying with a loud voice, Fear God, and give glory to him; for the hour of his judgment is come: and worship him that made heaven, and earth, and the sea, and the fountains of waters. And there followed another angel, saying, Babylon is fallen, is fallen, that great city, because she made all nations drink of the wine of the wrath of her fornication. And the third angel followed them, saying with a loud voice, If any man worship the beast and his image, and receive his mark in his forehead, or in his hand, The same shall drink of the wine of the wrath of God, which is poured out without mixture into the cup of his indignation; and he shall be tormented with fire and brimstone in the presence of the holy angels, and in the presence of the Lamb: And the smoke of their torment ascendeth up for ever and ever: and they have no rest day nor night, who worship the beast and his image, and whosoever receiveth the mark of his name. Here is the patience of the saints: here are they that keep the commandments of God, and the faith of Jesus.

Revelation 14:6–12 (KJV)

For as the lightning cometh out of the east, and shineth even unto the west; so shall also the coming of the Son of man be.

Matthew 24:27 (KJV

For as the lightning, that lighteneth out of the one part under heaven, shineth unto the

other part under heaven; so shall also the Son
of man be in his day.

Luke 17:24 (KJV)

And except those days should be shortened,
there should no flesh be saved: but for the
elect's sake those days shall be shortened.

Matthew 24:22 (KJV)

And he shall send his angels with a great
sound of a trumpet, and they shall gather
together his elect from the four winds, from
one end of heaven to the other.

Matthew 24:31 (KJV)

And then shall he send his angels, and shall
gather together his elect from the four winds,
from the uttermost part of the earth to the
uttermost part of heaven.

Mark 13:27 (KJV)

And he shall send his angels with a great
sound of a trumpet, and they shall gather

together his elect from the four winds, from one end of heaven to the other.

Matthew 24:31 (KJV)

In a moment, in the twinkling of an eye, at the last trump: for the trumpet shall sound, and the dead shall be raised incorruptible, and we shall be changed.

1 Corinthians 15:52 (KJV)

For the Lord himself will come down from heaven, with a loud command, with the voice of the archangel and with the trumpet call of God, and the dead in Christ will rise first. After that, we who are still alive and are left will be caught up together with them in the clouds to meet the Lord in the air. And so we will be with the Lord forever.

1 Thessalonians 4:16, 17 (KJV)

So speak ye, and so do, as they that shall be judged by the law of liberty.

James 2:12 (NIV)

## Conclusion

> At that time the sign of the Son of Man will
> appear in the sky, and all the nations of the
> earth will mourn. They will see the Son of
> Man coming on the clouds of the sky, with
> power and great glory. And he will send his
> angels with a loud trumpet call, and they will
> gather his elect from the four winds, from
> one end of the heavens to the other.
>
> Matthew 24: 30, 31 (KJV)

Following this present period of judgment and a
terrible time of trouble coming upon the inhabitants
of the earth, the Lord will return to receive his own.
This will be a visible, splendid, global event! Nothing
secret!

## Publish Outcomes

> Behold, I come quickly: blessed is he that
> keepeth the sayings of the prophecy of this
> book.
>
> Revelation 22:7 (KJV)

And he said unto them, Go ye into all the world, and preach the gospel to every creature.

Mark 16:15 (NIV)

He that hath an ear, let him hear what the Spirit saith unto the churches.

Revelation 3:22 (KJV)

Then I saw another angel flying in midair, and he had the eternal gospel to proclaim to those who live on the earth—to every nation, tribe, language and people. He said in a loud voice, "Fear God and give him glory, because the hour of his judgment has come. Worship him who made the heavens, the earth, the sea and the springs of water." A second angel followed and said, "Fallen! Fallen is Babylon the Great, which made all the nations drink the maddening wine of her adulteries." A third angel followed them and said in a loud voice: "If anyone worships the beast and his image and receives his mark on the forehead or on the hand, he, too, will drink of the wine of God's fury, which has been poured full strength into the cup of his wrath. He will be tormented with burning sulfur in the presence of the holy angels and of the Lamb. And the smoke of their torment rises for ever and ever. There is no rest day or night for those who worship the beast and his image, or for anyone who receives the mark of his name." This calls for patient endurance on the part of the saints who obey God's commandments and remain faithful to Jesus.

Revelation 14:6–12 (KJV)

And, behold, I come quickly; and my reward is with me, to give every man according as his work shall be.

Revelation 22:12

# Miracles and Blessings!

# References

Holy Bible King James Version
Holy Bible New International Version
Holy Bible New American Standard
Holy Bible New English Standard
Holy Bible New Living Translation
Holy Bible Amplified
www.Absoluteastronomy.com
www.Biblegateway.com
E-Sword

1. See "http://www.absoluteastronomy.com/topics" http:// www.absoluteastronomy.com/topics, for more information regarding the division of Greece after the death of Alexander

# e|LIVE

## listen|imagine|view|experience

### AUDIO BOOK DOWNLOAD INCLUDED WITH THIS BOOK!

In your hands you hold a complete digital entertainment package. Besides purchasing the paper version of this book, this book includes a free download of the audio version of this book. Simply use the code listed below when visiting our website. Once downloaded to your computer, you can listen to the book through your computer's speakers, burn it to an audio CD or save the file to your portable music device (such as Apple's popular iPod) and listen on the go!

How to get your free audio book digital download:

1. Visit www.tatepublishing.com and click on the e|LIVE logo on the home page.
2. Enter the following coupon code:
   872e-7366-2910-3ae7-cb0d-0bdd-402d-91eb
3. Download the audio book from your e|LIVE digital locker and begin enjoying your new digital entertainment package today!